J PAR STORYTIME KIT BOD

Bodies [storytime kit]
Total - 22 pieces

Bilingual Edition

Clean and Healthy / Limpieza y salud

Edición Bilingüe

Let's Exercise
¡A hacer ejercicio!

Elizabeth Vogel
Traducción al español:
Tomás González

The Rosen Publishing Group's
PowerKids Press™ & **Editorial Buenas Letras**™
New York

1

Published in 2001, 2004 by The Rosen Publishing Group, Inc.
29 East 21st Street, New York, NY 10010

First Bilingual Edition 2004
First Edition in English 2001

Book Design: Felicity Erwin
Layout: Dean Galiano

Photo Illustrations by Michelle Midura

Vogel, Elizabeth.
   Let's Exercice = ¡A hacer ejercicio! / by Elizabeth Vogel ; traducción al español Tomás González.
   p. cm.—(PowerKids Readers. Clean & Healthy All Day Long = Limpieza y salud todo el día)
   Includes bibliographical references and index.
   Summary: A boy describes ways of exercising every day and explains the benefits of physical fitness.
   ISBN 0-8239-6615-1
   1. Exercise—Juvenile literature. 2. Children—Health and hygiene—Juvenile literature. 3. Exercise for children—Juvenile literature. [1. Exercise. 2. Physical fitness. 3. Spanish language materials—Bilingual]
   I. Title. II. Series.
   613.7'1—dc21

Manufactured in the United States of America

Contents

Contenido

I exercise every day.

———

Hago ejercicio todos los días.

4

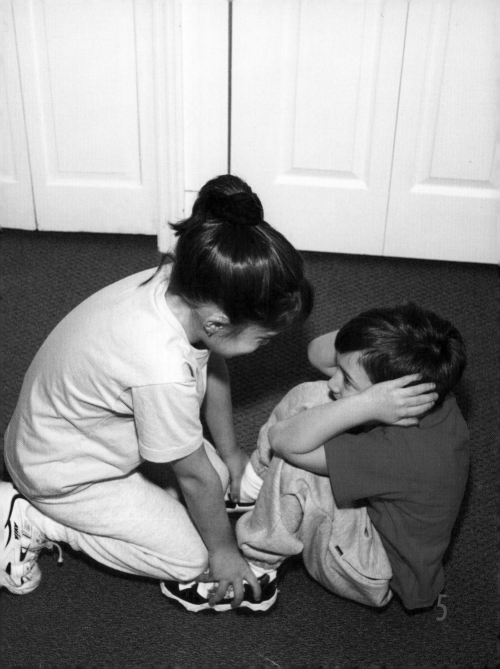

5

I want to be strong. I want to be healthy. Exercise helps make me strong. Exercise helps make me healthy.

Quiero ser fuerte. Quiero ser saludable. El ejercicio me hace fuerte. El ejercicio me hace saludable.

There are a lot of ways to exercise. You can play basketball. You can play baseball. You can jump rope.

———

Hay muchas formas de hacer ejercicio. Puedes jugar baloncesto. Puedes jugar béisbol. También puedes saltar la cuerda.

Exercise helps make your heart strong. Your heart is the size of a fist. The heart is the strongest muscle in the body.

El ejercicio te fortalece el corazón. Tu corazón es del tamaño del puño de una mano. El corazón es el músculo más fuerte del cuerpo.

I like to jump rope.
Jumping rope is good
exercise.

———————

Me gusta saltar la
cuerda. Saltar la cuerda
es buen ejercicio.

13

I clean my room. I walk around. I pick things up. Cleaning my room is good exercise.

———

Cuando limpio mi cuarto, camino por todas partes y recojo cosas. Limpiar mi cuarto es buen ejercicio.

I lift my arms up high. This stretches my muscles so they do not get hurt.

Levanto los brazos varias veces. Así estiro los músculos y no se lastiman con el ejercicio.

17

I throw a basketball in the air. I stretch my arms when I throw the basketball.

Lanzo al aire una pelota de baloncesto. Al lanzar la pelota estiro los brazos.

Exercise makes me healthy. It makes me happy, too!

———————

El ejercicio me hace saludable. ¡Y también me hace feliz!

Words to Know
Palabras que debes saber

BASEBALL /
BÉISBOL

BASKETBALL /
BALONCESTO

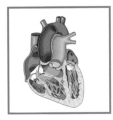

HEART /
CORAZÓN

JUMP ROPE /
CUERDA PARA SALTAR

MUSCLE /
MÚSCULO

STRETCH /
ESTIRAR

Here are more books to read about exercise / Otros libros que puedes leer sobre la alimentación sana:

In English/En inglés:
Fit Kids!: The Complete Shape-Up program from Birth Through High School
by Dr. Kenneth H. Cooper, Arnold Schwarzenegger, and William Proctor
Broadman & Holman Publishers

In Spanish/En español:
¿Estoy sano? Aprender sobre alimentación y actividad física. Colección Mi cuerpo y yo
Por Claire Llewellyn
Ed. Albatros, Buenos Aires, Argentina, 2000

Due to the changing nature of Internet links, PowerKids Press has developed an online list of Web sites related to the subject of this book. This site is updated regularly. Please use this link to access the list:

http://www.buenasletraslinks.com/chl/le

Index

Índice

Words in English: 135   Palabras en español: 131

Note to Parents, Teachers, and Librarians

PowerKids Readers en Español are specially designed to get emergent and beginning hispanic readers excited about learning to read. Simple stories and concepts are paired with photographs of real kids in real-life situations. Sentences are short and simple, employing a basic vocabulary of sight words, as well as new words that describe familiar things and places. With their engaging stories and vivid photo-illustrations, PowerKids en Español gives children the opportunity to develop a love of reading and learning that they will carry with them throughout their lives.

24